Martial

SELECTED EPIGRAMS

The Library of Liberal Arts

Martial

SELECTED EPIGRAMS

TRANSLATED

WITH AN INTRODUCTION

BY RALPH MARCELLINO

The Library of Liberal Arts

Published by

THE BOBBS-MERRILL COMPANY, INC.

A Subsidiary of Howard W. Sams & Co., Inc.

Indianapolis · New York

To My Wife

CONTENTS

Introduction

Marcus Valerius Martialis, whom Lessing called "the greatest epigrammatist who ever lived," was born a Roman citizen about A.D. 40 in Bilbilis, Spain. In A.D. 64, when he was in his early twenties, he left Bilbilis for Rome; there, no doubt, he immediately sought the aid and patronage of his fellow Spaniards Seneca and Lucan. But their assistance lasted only for a short time: on Nero's orders, they were forced to end their lives because of their alleged connection the previous year with the Pisonian conspiracy, aimed at the Emperor's assassination. Little is known about Martial during the next fifteen years, except that he lived in a dreary third-floor apartment in the heart of the city.

In 80 or so, Martial published his first book of epigrams, the *Liber Spectaculorum* (see p. 152), a work designed to celebrate the opening of the Flavian Amphitheater (better known as the Colosseum) and the many spectacles held there during the celebration. Four or five years later there appeared two collections of epigrams, now numbered Books XIII (*Xenia*) and XIV (*Apophoreta*). These contained 350 elegiac couplets—"cracker mottoes," as Mackail scoffingly calls them[1]—written to embellish gifts given during the Saturnalia in December (pp. 149–151). At about the same time, Martial acquired the Nomentanum, the country home he enjoyed so much for the escape it afforded him from Rome—although he constantly poked fun at its failings as a farm (pp. 97, 104, 124)—and a city house somewhere on the Quirinal. His major work, the twelve books of epigrams, began to appear in about A.D. 86, early in the reign of Domitian; from then on until about 96, Martial published a volume of epigrams almost every year. In 98, disgusted with the Rome he

1. *Latin Literature* (London: John Murray, 1909), p. 193.

once loved so much, Martial went back to Bilbilis, never to return to Rome. The decision to leave Rome for Spain he soon regretted.[2] In Bilbilis he produced one more volume of epigrams (Book XII), which was published in Rome about 101–102; shortly thereafter (ca. 104), Martial died.

So for about 35 years Martial had lived in Rome, that city of marvels, "the hub of the Globe," "the inn of the world." There he sat and studied, or mingled with, the most heterogeneous people in the world: the high, the low, the rich, the poor, the true, the pretenders, the prostitutes, the homosexuals, the parasites, the legacy-hunters, the writers, the would-be writers, the honest, the dishonest, the healthy and the sick, the farmers and the city-dwellers, the stingy and the generous—the whole panorama of the society that constituted the capital of the world. All of these people, Romans and strangers, Martial wrote about in his epigrams.

Either because he had no talent for epic poetry and tragedy, or because these forms—tragedy in particular—concerned themselves with mythology and its incredible characters and events, Martial wrote about real people, about contemporary men and manners. And he did it with the craftsmanship of a great artist, employing exclusively the epigram, a genre which he brought to perfection. "Martial," says C. A. Ker,[3] "at his best

2. "I miss that audience of my fellow-citizens to which I had grown accustomed, and seem to myself a pleader in a strange court; for whatever is popular in my small books my hearer inspired. That subtlety of judgment, that inspiration of the subject, the libraries, theatres, meeting-places, where pleasure is a student without knowing it—to sum up all, those things which fastidiously I deserted I regret, like one desolate. Added to this is the back-biting of my fellow-townsmen, and envy ousting judgment, and one or other evilly disposed persons—a host in a tiny place—a circumstance against which it is difficult every day to keep a good stomach. . . ." *Martial Epigrams*, tr. Walter C. A. Ker, "The Loeb Classical Library" (Cambridge, Mass.: Harvard University Press, 1961), II, 317.

3. *Ibid.*, I, xiii.

is without rival. If the highest form of art be to conceal art, then he was a consummate artist. The point, whether dependent on a pun, or an ambiguous phrase, on a new meaning given to a word, or an antithesis, or παρὰ προδοκίαν, is sharply brought out. And the words fall into their places with a fitness that suggests the solution of a puzzle: the reader feels that no other words could have been employed."

Pliny said of Martial that he wrote with the hope and the conviction that his work would last forever. And it has.

The nucleus of this collection is a slim volume of 47 poems which appeared in March, 1963; it was then called *The Pensive and the Antic Muse*. The title indicates its intent: to show the serious as well as the humorous or satiric side of Martial; for, judging by the translations which had appeared sporadically over the years, and which still appear in learned journals, it is always Martial the wit who is attempted, and seldom Martial, the writer of serious poetry. The balance of the original volume, therefore, has been maintained in this larger collection also.

In the translations which follow, I have in every case employed stanzaic form and rhyme, convinced that an epigram needs form and rhyme to make the poem or its point memorable and quotable. The meters I have used are quite varied: the tone, the spirit, the subject of the Latin have determined the formal characteristics of the translation. Above all, it has been the point and how best to express it that have determined the meter and the stanzaic form, for if the point fails in translation there is no excuse for attempting the poem at all.

Since a poem is more than the words it contains, I have not hesitated to translate the words between the lines when necessary, always for the sake of comprehensibility. I have often resorted to glozing, too, again for the sake of comprehensibility because if a translation employing twentieth-century language is not immediately understandable, it is a bore and a failure. This practice has resulted in a certain amount of expansion—the kind of expansion which Professor W. F. Jackson Knight uses in his remarkable translation of the *Aeneid*.

Finally, I wish to acknowledge the close and expert reading of the manuscript of these translations by Professor Frank O. Copley, who offered very valuable suggestions and made some corrections.

Ralph Marcellino

Selected Bibliography

BUTLER, H. E. *Post-Augustan Poetry*. Oxford, 1909.

CARCOPINO, J. *Daily Life in Ancient Rome*. Tr. E. O. Lorimer. New Haven: Yale University Press, 1940.

DILL, S. *Roman Society from Nero to Marcus Aurelius*. London: Macmillan, 1904.

DUFF, J. W. *A Literary History of Rome in the Silver Age*. New York: Charles Scribner's Sons, 1927. Chapter VII, "Martial and Minor Flavian Poetry."

FRIEDLÄNDER, L. *Roman Life and Manners Under the Early Empire*. Tr. Leonard A. Magnus. 7th edition. Vol. IV (Appendices). London: George Routledge & Sons, 1928.

FRIEDLÄNDER, L. *The Epigrams of Martial*, with explanatory notes. 2 vols. Leipzig, 1886.

GREENIDGE, A. H. J. *Roman Public Life*. London: Macmillan, 1931.

GWYNN, A. *Roman Education from Cicero to Quintilian*. Oxford: Clarendon Press, 1926.

IZAAC, H. J. *Martial: Epigrammes*. Text and French translation. 2 vols. Paris: Société D'Edition, "Les Belles Lettres," 1961.

JOHNSTON, H. W. *The Private Life of the Romans*. Rev. by Mary Johnston. New York: Scott, Foresman & Co., 1932.

KER, WALTER C. A., tr. *Martial: Epigrams*. "The Loeb Classical Library." Cambridge, Mass.: Harvard University Press, 1946.

MACKAIL, J. W. *Latin Literature*. London: John Murray, 1909.

MATTINGLY, H. *The Man in the Roman Street*. New York: *The Numismatic Review*, 1947.

MCKAY, A. G. *Naples and Campania*. Ontario: The Vergilian Society of America, 1962.

NIXON, P. *Martial and the Modern Epigram*. New York: Cooper Square Publishers, Inc., 1963.

PECK, H. T., ed. *Harper's Dictionary of Classical Literature and Antiquities*. 2nd edn. New York: American Book Co., 1897.

POST, E., ed. *Selected Epigrams of Martial*. New York: Ginn & Co., 1908.

Pott, J. A., and F. A. Wright. *Martial, the Twelve Books of Epigrams.* London and New York, 1926.

Showerman, G. *Rome and the Romans.* New York: Macmillan, 1931.

Smith, W. *Dictionary of Antiquities.* London, 1890–1891.

Stephenson, H. M. *Selected Epigrams of Martial,* ed. with notes. London, 1880.

Tyrrell, R. Y. *Latin Poetry.* London: Macmillan, 1895. Pages 285–289.

Walters, H. B. *A Classical Dictionary of Greek and Roman Antiquities, Biography, Geography, and Mythology.* Cambridge: University Press, 1916.

Martial

SELECTED EPIGRAMS

To the Reader

Here's that famous Martial, reader,
　　The poet you've been asking for,
Known throughout the universe
　　For his bright and witty store.

On him, dear reader, you've bestowed,
　　While he's alive and bold of breath,
That immortality reserved
　　For just a few—and after death.

To His Public

You who've craved to have my poems
  With you always, night and day,
And you who seek a book companion
  For your journey far away,
Buy this neatly published offering,
  Pocket-sized, light but strong,
And leave those huge, those heavy volumes
  On their shelves where they belong.
And lest you should not know the bookshop
  Where it's sold, and far and wide
Wander lost throughout the city,
  Let me be your helpful guide:
Seek the publisher Secundus,
  Lucensis' slave once, now set free;
Close behind Minerva's Forum
  And that of Peace, his shop you'll see.

On Gemellus

Maronilla is the girl
   He yearns to wed.
And so determined is the lover
   That, it's said,
He sues and courts her ardently
   Both day and night
And heaps upon her gifts that would
   Amaze the sight.
Is she then so attractive? Tell me.
   Heavens, no!
There's nothing uglier in all
   The world to show.
Then what's she got that clears up this
   Great mystery?
Plenty of money and a cough
   That spells T. B.

To Avitus

Some of these epigrams are good,
    Some mediocre, many bad.
Otherwise, it is understood,
    A bookful of poems cannot be had.

To Cotta

The only ones you ask to dine
    Are those you meet at public baths.
Only in such institutions
    Comes this crossing of your paths.

I used to wonder why you never
    Asked me home to dine with you.
Now I know: my naked body's
    Not attractive, in your view.

To Faustinus

Faustinus, why not publish them,
  Those masterpieces of a mind
Which Athens cannot but commend,
  To which Rome cannot but be kind?

Tell me why you hesitate;
  Fame is standing at your door.
Take the prize she long has offered,
  Long has held for you in store!

Let works that will survive you after
  You have trod the path so dread
Live now, while you still are living.
  Fame comes too late to the dead.

To Procillus

Last night I said, while feeling fine,
Having drunk much too much wine,

That you must promise, when this way,
To stop and dine with me some day.

You made a mental note of it,
A practice which, I must admit—

Taking me at my drunken word!—
Is dangerous and quite absurd.

Barroom promises are fine,
But he who keeps them is a swine!

On Acerra

You say he still reeked of last night's wine
  When he spoke to you, stifling a yawn?
Oh no, you are wrong, you're mistaken, sir!
  He always drinks till dawn.

To Linus

He who says, "Forget it! Keep it!"
    Outright giving you
Half of what you wish to borrow
    Is in my own view
Shrewd as well as generous:
    He'd rather take a fall
And *give* you half the sum you wish
    Than lend—and lose it all!

To Novius, Who Is Always Out
Visiting Distant Friends

He's my neighbor, lives so near
That from my window where I stand
I can touch him with my hand.

Everybody envies me,
Thinks me fortunate no end
Living near so close a friend.

Yet, he is actually as far
As Terence is (you need not smile),
And *he*, you know, lives on the Nile.

I never see him, never hear him,
Never meet him at the bar,
This friend so near and yet so far.

One of us must move away.
He who does not wish to see
Novius must his neighbor be.

(I. 86)

To Laelius

Although you have not published
    Even a single line
Of poetry yourself, you scoff
    And sneer and jeer at mine.
Get off my back or publish!
    I'd like to hear you whine!

To Lucius Julius

My dearest Julius, this is what
    You tell me constantly:
"For heaven's sake, write something great!
    How lazy can you be?"

Give me the leisure Virgil had,
    The leisure that Maecenas
Gave Horace, too, and we'll essay
    Our utmost to redeem us

In your cold eyes. We'll write a work
    To last for generations,
A work that will defy the wrack
    Of time's swift depredations.

A bullock scorns to waste his strength
    On sandy, sterile soil.
A rich field tires him, but delights
    And challenges his toil.

On His Work

He who's read one hundred of
   These epigrams of mine
And still reads on unsatiated
   Is, I think, the kind
Of reader who can never be
Glutted with mediocrity.

To His Friend, Decianus

"Why don't you call and stay a while?"
    I'd love to, thank you. Fine!
But it's two miles from door to door
    And four round-trip to mine.

I do call, and you're often out;
    If in, you're "not at home"—
Busy with some client, or
    Deep in some legal tome.

I don't mind chancing those two miles
    That take me to your door
To see you, but to see you *not*
    I do mind trudging four.

To His Reader

Dear reader, if you find herein
   Poems that are obscure
Or written in an idiom
   You'd scarce consider pure,

The fault's not mine. The blame belongs
   Entirely on the printer,
Who rushed to put this volume out
   Before the approach of winter.

But if, dear reader, you insist
   The fault's not his, but mine,
I must presume you are obtuse,
   Or utterly unkind.

Still you protest how bad they are;
   I answer, "What the hell!
Some are quite bad, but do you think
   That you could do as well?"

To Postumus

How to explain? Your kisses smell
    Of something sweet, like myrrh.
Around you there's an odor that's
    Exotic, as it were.

A man who always smells so sweet,
    The way you always do,
Is suspect. No one can smell nice
    Who smells as nice as you.

To Postumus Again

Some of your friends you kiss;
    Others you shake by the hand.
You say to me: "Which do you wish?
    Choose! You have but to command!"
Knowing your practices, sir,
    Your hand is what *I* would prefer.

To Apollo and the Muses

Ye sisters nine, Apollo, too,
What have I done to anger you?
The antic Muse, my former friend,
Gives me suffering no end:
There was a time when Postumus kissed
With listless lips, and always missed.
But now with hungry mouth he seeks
And finds my poor, reluctant cheeks!

On Postumus Again

I can't reveal, however much
    You ask me to, the name,
The real name of this Postumus
    Of such unsavory fame.

I can't reveal it. Why should I
    Offend those osculations
Which can so well avenge themselves
    Upon the revelation?

To Galla

You always promise, never give.
  You live but to confuse!
If you must always be so false,
  I beg you to refuse!

(II. 25)

To Linus

You don't see what I see, you say,
In living here so far away?
What I see, Linus, is a view
In which I see no sign of you.

To Zoïlus in His Bath

Why do you waste that water, getting
    Merely your bottom wet?
To wash the real filth off, Monsieur,
    Submergez votre tête!

Spatale at the Bathhouse Gate

Though it was wide, so wide was she,
   So huge she barely made it.
The guard demanded a triple fee,
   And she, that mountain, paid it!

To Nasica

You ask me over the very same day
   On which you know I've invited
Others for supper. Excuse me, but
   I'm dining at home (and delighted)!

(II. 79)

To Quintilian

O famous curb of wayward youth,
    Rome's most renowned civilian,
Forgive my hastening to live
    Before I've made my million—
Though I am poor enough and strong
To keep on working right along.

One can't begin to live too soon!
    Let him defer it who has
Grand designs on marble halls
    Crammed with works by Scopas,
And who desires even more
Than his father had before.

For me enough's a fireplace,
    A home that does not mind
The smoke, a spring, a plot of ground,
    A maid, a wife (the kind
Not overlearned), dreamless nights,
And days devoid of legal fights.

(II. 90)

To Gallus

You never ask me to your home,
 Though often asked to mine.
I wouldn't mind it if you asked
 No others home to dine.

But you do ask these others; so
 I guess we're both to blame.
How so? I must have little sense,
 And you no sense of shame.

On a Vase

See this Phidian vase.
   Carved upon its brim
Are fish in high relief.
   Add water, and they swim.

To Faustinus

One-eyed Lycoris loves a boy
   As fair as Ganymede
The Trojan. Say, this one-eyed girl
   Sees very well indeed!

(III. 39)

On a Silver Cup

Embossed by Mentor on this cup
A lizard sleeps so very real
One fears to put his hand near it;
One hesitates to touch or feel.

To Ligurinus

Whether Apollo fled in haste
    Thyestes' banquet table,
I don't know, but I do know this:
    Not one of us is able
To stomach yours. It's true it's grand,
    An epicure's delight,
But then you bore us with those lines
    You feel you must recite.
You do not need to serve us turbots,
    Two-pound mullets or
Mushrooms or oysters. All we want
    Is this: recite no more!

(III. 45)

To Galla

When I praise your face and lovely hands
    Or to your legs allude,
This is what you always say:
    "I'm nicer in the nude."

And yet you constantly decline
    To go to the Baths with me.
Are you afraid you'll be displeased
    With my own nudity?

To Chloe

Chloe, I can do without
    Your face, dear, and your lips,
Your neck, your hands, your breasts, your thighs,
    Your buttocks, and your hips.

In short, my dear, I can dispense
    With quite an awful lot.
In fact, I can dispense with, Chloe,
    Everything you've got.

To Galla

Because the price you ask
  Is more than I can pay,
You'd save me much embarrassment
  With just a "Not today."

Ravenna

In water-starved Ravenna
    I'd rather own a well
Than vineyards. Water's scarce, and far
    More lucrative to sell.

The Innkeeper at Ravenna

There's an innkeeper at Ravenna
  Who is an arrant cheat.
I asked for wine with water;
  He served it to me neat!

To Cassianus

Those songstresses, the Sirens
   (Those tuneful maidens whom
No passing sailors could resist,
   Their joy and merry doom),
Wily Ulysses, so they say,
Heard unharmed and went his way.

I'm not surprised. I would be, though,
   If he could so prevail
As to escape from Canius
   And his alluring tales.

To Apicius

No evil or abusive word,
   No word that ever stung
Dropped from his lips, and yet he had,
   They say, a shameful tongue.

To Rufus

You threaten to whip your bungling cook
    Because the hare is rare.
You'd rather cut up the cook, of course,
    Than have to share the hare.

To Thais

Thais, you don't refuse yourself
    To any man you meet!
Now, if you're not ashamed of that,
    Then blush for this, at least
(For it should cause your face to sting):
    You don't refuse them anything!

On Segius

"There are no gods, and heaven's all a lie!
    No gods," said Segius, "give a damn or care
What happens to us." And he must be right:
    Today the rat's a multi-millionaire.

To a Would-Be Poet

Why do you put a scarf around your neck
   When you recite? The strain? Allay your fears!
Your voice has never faltered, never yet.
   I wish I had that scarf—around my ears!

On the Eruption of Vesuvius

Behold Vesuvius lately green
　　With vineyard-covered slopes!
Here did the noble grapevine yield
　　Beyond one's wildest hopes!

Here are the ridges Bacchus loved
　　More than those of his youth.
And here till late his Satyrs danced
　　Their merry dance uncouth.

Here stood Pompeii, dearer far
　　To Aphrodite than
The Lacedaemonian island where
　　Her early life began.

And here stood Herculaneum,
　　Founded by Hercules
When here he paused to rest the oxen
　　Of Geryones.

All this, by fire and flame consumed,
　　Lies sunk, so sad a sight
The very gods might wish they had
　　Not had it in their might.

To Flaccus

He does not know what epigrams
    Are really meant to be
Who calls them only jests and jokes
    Or comic poetry—
A dimwit dilettante's delight,
    Mere *vers de societé.*

He really is the one who jests
    Who writes about the stew
Served Tereus, or that loathsome meal
    Of children served to you,
Thyestes, indigestion-prone,
    Of sons your brother slew,

Or Daedalus fitting Icarus
    With two liquescent wings,
Or who of Polyphemus tending
    Sheep in Sicily sings,
And those huge, monstrous boulders which
    He at Ulysses flings.

Far from my verse is any trace
    Of rank turgidity.
My Muse has never donned the robes
    Of pompous tragedy.
"But that's what's praised!" But what is read?
    My earthy poetry!

To Collinus

O you on whom was first bestowed
The Emperor's oak-leaf crown of gold,
If wise, Collinus, you'd essay
To live each minute of each day
As though it were your very last—
As it may be! Your fate holds fast!
To no one has it ever been
Allowed to slow the hands that spin.
The Sisters, in grim business met,
Keep the final day they've set.
Even were you richer than
Crispus, that most wealthy man,
More virtuous in all your life
Than Paetus and his blameless wife,
Were you even handsomer
Than most young men, a Melior,
Still would all this nothing prove,
Still would you fail her heart to move
Who pulls and measures out the thread
Her sister cuts. And all is said.

(IV. 54)

To Papilus

I see you do serve Massic wine
    And even glorious Setian.
But rumor has it that they smack
    A bit of that Venetian
Mixture that Lucretia served,
    That four of your dear wives
On tasting those expensive labels
    Promptly lost their lives.
It's all, I'm sure, a lot of talk,
    Incredible, I think.
But thank you, no; I've got to go.
    Besides, I do not drink.

To Safronius Rufus

I've searched throughout the city for
    A girl who can say no,
And haven't found a single one!
    They all behave as though
It's impolite or shameful or
    Unlawful to refuse.
Is there no living girl that's chaste,
    No girl one can't accuse
Of frailty? "There are a thousand!"
    Rufus, it is not so!
All chaste girls will consent when asked.
    When *not* asked, they say no!

To Fabulla

When Fabulla read the poem in which
    I claimed no girl says no,
She coldly spurned my hot advances
    Three times in a row.

Promise you'll drop this silliness!
    The point, Fabulla, never
In bidding girls refuse us men
    Was to refuse forever!

(IV. 81)

On Phasis

While Phasis in the theater recently
   (Phasis, the pompous pheasant in purple clothes)
Lauded the edict of our Emperor
   And God, whereby the choice orchestral rows
Of seats are now officially reserved
   For only those who rank as Roman Knights;
While proudly and quite loudly he proclaimed
   That "Now at last our just equestrian rights
Have been restored and all our dignity,
   No longer need we suffer the *canaille*
To push and shove us"; while these observations
   He made reclining, Leïtus came by,
Tapped the arrant knave as there he sat,
And ordered him to lift his plumes and scat.

To Doctor Symmachus

I wasn't really sick at all,
   Just felt a little weak
When you appeared with your one hundred
   Boys to see the "freak."

A hundred clammy, cold hands touched me,
   A hundred felt my brow.
I didn't have a fever then,
   But I sure have one now!

To Regulus

Why is fame the living denied?
Why are modern times decried
So much? The answer, Regulus,
Is: That is the way of the envious.
They much prefer the old, the dead.
The new is not accredited.
That's why ingrates seek the shade
Of Pompey's ancient colonnade.
That's why old folks still adore
That temple Catulus restored.
The works of Ennius still were read,
O Rome, when Virgil was not yet dead.
They laughed at Homer in those days
When Homer wrote. Menander's plays
Seldom reached the Attic stage
And won applause. In Ovid's age
Only Corinna hailed the birth
Of Ovid's works and knew their worth.

Impatient little books of verse
For the plaudits of the universe,
If fame comes only after death,
Let's pause and rest, and catch our breath.

To Callistratus

I am, and I have always been
    (Let's get the story right!)
A poor, but never an obscure
    Or unknown Roman Knight.
Avid readers scan my books
    Everywhere. Constantly
They point in admiration, saying,
    "Look! Look! That is he!"
And fame which death has given few
    On me has been conferred
While still alive.   In your case, now,
    A hundred columns serve
To lift your roof. Your strongbox holds
    A freedman's massive treasure.
Your vast estates along the Nile
    Yield profits past all measure.
Your countless flocks of sheep in Gaul
    Supply wool endlessly.
You can't be what I am. You are
    What any fool can be.

To the Emperor Domitian

Your Majesty, behold another
   Book of antic verses!
And no one's yet cried, "It's a lie!"
   Or heaped my head with curses.
Many a reader, Sir, in fact,
   Delights to see his name
(Thanks to these lines of mine) achieve
   Imperishable fame.
"What good to you can these lines do,
   Whomever they may flatter?"
Granted they bring no riches in,
   They please me. That's what matters.

To Gellia

While fathers of great-grandfathers
    And all their famous names
You boasted of, and snorted at
    My proud equestrian claims,
Yes, while you said no one could wed
    So pedigreed a daughter
Save royalty or senators,
    You hitched up with a porter!

To His Friend, Martial

If, my dear Martial, it were in our power
To live enjoying fully every hour,
Unplagued by the petty cares that mar our day,
If we were free to spend in our own way
What leisure time we had, if we could be
Allowed the life we yearn for fervidly,
We would not have to court the great, the proud,
We would not have to visit with the crowd
Those stately homes, those lofty domiciles,
We would not know the meanness and the wiles
Which lawyers practice in the glittering forum,
Saddening for all its pretense of decorum.
Instead we'd spend our time in promenades,
In conversation in cool colonnades,
In talk of books, in gentle exercise
At public baths. All these, if we were wise,
Would be the places we would most frequent;
These the tasks that most would suit our bent.
But as things now are, neither one of us
Lives for himself, while ever glorious
Days slip by unlived, never to come
Again, deducted always from that sum
Allotted us. Why then do we not live,
We who know the joys that life can give?

To a Would-Be Knight

That the air, the taste, the manners, even the blood
  Of knighthood are yours, I won't deny;
But not the income. There you're hoi polloi.
  It isn't worth your while to occupy
A knight's seat, if you must sit there in fear
Lest usher Oceanus should come near.

To Aulus on Mamercus

There is no art whereby you can
    Induce Mamercus, none,
To speak or think, dear Aulus, well
    Or kindly of anyone.
Even if you could surpass
    In love and piety
The brothers Curvius, and Nerva
    In equanimity,
Ruso in his friendliness,
    In justice Mauricus,
Macer my friend in probity,
    In discourse Regulus,
Paulus in wit, he'll snap at you
    And everyone he can.
Malicious would you call him? No!
    A lone, unhappy man!

On the Child Erotion

To thee, my father, and to thee, my mother,
   I recommend this darling little maid.
Shield her from that dreadful hound of Hades,
   Shield her from the dark infernal shades.
She would have known the chill of six cold winters
   Had she lived only six more little days.
Amid such old defenders let her frolic
   And babble my name as was her childish way.
Lie lightly on her, earth, O lie not heavy
   Upon her bones, for she was light on thee.

To Faustinus

A certain man, Faustinus, whom
I praised once in my book
Pretends he's not in debt to me
For anything, the crook!

(V. 36)

To Charinus and His Coffin Cough

Every time you were about
  To write your will last year
(That happened only thirty times!)
  I sent you gifts to cheer
Your feeble state—expensive cakes
  Steeped in Hyblaean honey.
Result? I'm broke! Sign rarerly!
  It's cost me all my money!
Or else at long last do that thing
  Your lying cough suggests
Repeatedly—give up and die,
  And give my purse a rest.
My safe deposit box is bare;
  My wallet's empty, too.
Had I another Croesus been,
  I would be poorer now
Than beggar Irus whom we see
In Homer's tale, the *Odyssey*—
Had you as often sponged and dined
On what I eat—cheap beans and wine.

To Didymus

Although you're more effeminate
  Than a soft, castrated male,
More womanish than Attis was—
  That concubine bewailed
By those emasculated priests
  Of Mother Cybele—
You talk of theater seats and bans,
  The equestrian holiday,
Of purple gowns with jeweled clasps,
  Of wealth, and point a hand
As smoothly pumiced as a maid's
  At the vast, impoverished band.
Now whether you deserve to sit
  With knights, I'll tell you when
I've checked. Those other places are
  Reserved for married men.

A False Impression

Thais's teeth are black;
    Laecania's, snowy white.
The former has her own, of course;
    The latter—well, not quite.

To a Crass Procrastinator

"Tomorrow. I will live tomorrow,"
    That's what you always say.
But when will that tomorrow come?
    It did not come today!

How far away is that tomorrow?
    Just where can it be found?
In Parthia, Armenia,
    Some other distant ground?

All those tomorrows must have beards
    As long as that of Priam.
How much do those tomorrows cost?
    Where can a poor man buy 'em?

Gaudeamus, Postume,
    Iuvenes dum sumus.
Postumus, to live tomorrow
    Is to live *post humus!*

Yes, that is what wise Martial says,
    Though in another way:
"It's much too late today to live!
    The wise lived yesterday!"

(V. 58)

To His Slaves

Pour in an extra cup of dark Falernian.
    Strain it through the summer's snow and chill.
Anoint my dripping hair with fragrant perfume,
    And crown my head with roses, if you will.

The Mausoleum of divine Augustus
    Looming close, so very close nearby,
Orders us to live and love existence
    Since even gods themselves decline and die.

(V. 64)

Procne

When those Attic birds, the swallows,
    Flew off to their winter home
As is their way, one lonely bird
    Stayed on in her nest alone,

Where she remained unnoticed
    Until the birds next spring
Flew back again, and, maddened,
    Tore her wing from wing.

She paid the penalty, but too late.
They should have visited this fate
Upon the guilty mother when
She slew her lone child, there and then.

To Cinna, Latter-Day Mithridates

By taking poison every day
    A famous king succeeded
In rendering himself immune
    To any poison needed
By friendly foe or faithless friend
To bring His Highness to an end.

And so you, too, O Cinna, have
    Performed an equal feat:
By dining poorly every day
    You've learned how not to eat
To live, and so you'll never die
Of hunger—as may Dick or I.

To Aemilianus

Poor if you are, my friend,
    Poor will you always be.
Money gets money today;
    Poverty, poverty.

To Dindymus

You follow, I flee; you flee, I follow.
    That's the way it goes.
I hate your yeses, Dindymus.
    I much prefer your noes.

To Caecilianus

I've purchased a farm at a fabulous price.
    Will you lend me the thousand I lack?
I can tell by your silence you've said to yourself,
    "But you'll never pay me it back!"
If that's what you fear, that was my idea.
    Will you lend me the thousand I lack?

(VI. 5)

To His Lawyer

The charge is not assault or murder,
    Nor is it poisoning, you quack!
It's simply larceny: my neighbor
    Stole three goats which I want back!

Prove that, and to hell with Carthage,
    Cannae, the Mithridatic War,
Sulla, Marius, and Mucius!
    Speak the speech I'm paying for.

Drop the bombast! Please stop beating
    The air and yourself to a livid hue!
Stick to the subject, which is goats, sir,
    Those things, you know, that smell—like you.

(VI. 19)

To Caecilianus, Orator

The seven water clocks you asked for
    Loud and lustily
The judge, Caecilianus, granted
    Most unwillingly.

And since you are a windy man
    And, too, a thirsty ass
And drink the water, now lukewarm,
    From pitchers made of glass,

There is a way to quench for good
    That thirst and that great stock
Of endless words inside you, sir.
    Drink up the water clock!

(VI. 35)

To Lycoris on Glycera

There was no one but you once.
　　There's now no one but her.
She now, as you could too once,
　　Has all of me astir.
The years that pass, and with them
　　The changes that occur!
I was in love with you once.
　　I'm now in love with her.

To a Poet

He who gets up to recite,
　　His neck in a woolen wrap,
Tells us plainly he can neither
　　Speak nor shut his trap.

(VI. 41)

To Pomponius

The loud applause your speech received
    Was not at all deserved.
It was not the speech you gave we liked,
    But the dinner that you served.

(VI. 48)

To Bithynicus

When Telesinus was impoverished
And cultivated only honest men,
He walked about a shabby, filthy figure
And shivered in a flimsy toga. Then
When he took up with perverts, queers, and such
He suddenly, alone of all of us,
Bought silver plate, expensive furniture,
And landed homes at prices fabulous.
If you want wealth, become a man immoral.
A wealthy saint's a thing anomalous.

(VI. 50)

To Auctioneer, Gellianus

An auctioneer just lately tried to sell
A girl of not too good repute, a belle
Like one of those that sit in the Subura.
And since for long the price that would secure her
Was low, and small the profit he would glean,
To prove to all that she was truly clean,
He pulled her face to his, though she resisted,
And two times, three times, four times roundly kissed it.
Now what effect had this upon the sale?
The high man in disgust turned deadly pale,
And dropped his bid.

Caelia

Do you ask me why this girl prefers
   Eunuchs, that race defiled?
She'd rather get her fill of sex
   Than fill her belly with child.

(VI. 67)

To Pontilianus

You ask me why I do not send you
    All my latest publications?
Lest in turn you send me, sir,
    All your latest lucubrations!

To the Statue of the Running Boy, Argynnus

What boy is this who flees Ianthis' spring
And its bright waters? Hylas, running from
Its Naiad mistress? Lucky indeed you are
That Hercules is worshiped not afar
And from those woods guards well their amorous waters!
So stay, Argynnus. Boldly tend the spring.
Fear not the Naiads. They'll not do you harm;
Beware, if wise, the god who guards these quarters!

On a Fragment of the Ship Argo

This wooden fragment which you carelessly
    Pass by as of no great import, and cheap,
Is all that's left of that most famous ship,
    The first that dared to try the unknown deep.

This was the Argo, which the Clashing Rocks,
    The dread Symplegades, once failed to smash,
Which even the stormy Euxine's maddened waves,
    Hard though they struck, were powerless to crash.

Only the heavy weight of passing years
    Has conquered it. And only this remains:
A fragment, true, but far more precious now
    Than when, a ship, it leaped forth at the reins.

To Polla, on the Occasion
of Lucan's Birthday

This is that day which conscious of
   The marvel it had unfurled
Gave a beloved spouse to you
   And a poet to the world.

Ah, cruel Nero, none so hated,
   So much despised as you!
This murderous deed should not have been
   Within your power to do!

To Priscus

To give your gift an added lift
    You like to send with it verses
That will outlive the *Iliad*,
    The *Odyssey*, too, but (curses!)
Your muse is dumb, or will not come,
    Or else you're just a duffer.
Though you beat your brains with all the pains
    You take, it's we who suffer.
Send rich men verses. They, I'm sure,
    Will gain from them the lift
We hungry poor cannot secure.
    Give up! Just send the gift!

(VII. 46)

A Far-Flung Friend

You have one home on the Esquiline,
Another on the Aventine,

And from a third one you can see
The shrine of widowed Cybele.

From still another you've a view
Of both the temples, old and new,

Of Jupiter. In fact, a home
Of yours lies everywhere in Rome!

Where can I find you when in town?
At what address can you be found?

He who lives all over Rome
Never can be found at home.

To Lausus

Some thirty poems in this book
   Are poor, you say. Egad!
If you've found thirty good ones, too,
   The book is great, not bad.

To Sabellus

The fact that you can write with taste
    A quatrain now and then
And even several couplets too
    Is something I do commend,
But I'm not amazed, for after all
    A few epigrams smart and neat
Are easy to write, but a bookful of them
    Is quite another feat!

(VII. 85)

To Creticus

Matho exults and crows my book's uneven.
  If that is true, he praises me. I'm glad.
Calvinus and Umber write books that are even.
  Even books are books that are all bad.

To Cinna, a Tedious Lawyer

Is this the way to plead a case?
   Is this what you call eloquence?
To utter nine words! Nine! Within
   Ten hours—and all at my expense!

And just now in a thunderous voice
   You asked more time for your defense!
More time for further speechlessness!
   More time for mute grandiloquence!

(VIII. 7)

On Bassus

Bassus picked up a cloak of late,
    A Tyrian of the finest hue,
And worth ten thousand cesterces—
    A bargain, in my humble view.
"Did he get it cheap?" you say.
He did. He doesn't intend to pay.

On Rich Wives

You ask me why I do not care
    To wed a dame that's rich?
Because I then would be the woman;
    She, a male-souled bitch.

A wife must be inferior to
    Her man. I firmly state it!
Not otherwise can man and wife
    Be evenly matched and mated.

To Varus, Poet

Although you write two hundred lines
    Of poetry each day,
You shun our constant plea to let us
    Hear your poetry.

Two hundred verses every day,
    And I, with luck, one line!
You can't be good, though very good
    Of you, sir, to decline!

On His Cook

I know I seem quite gluttonous
    And certainly too cruel
For having struck my cook for serving
    This vile-tasting gruel.

If you deem the cause too trivial—
    A meal that can't be eaten!—
For what other reason do you think
    A bad cook should be beaten?

(VIII. 23)

To Oppianus

You called on me but once, when I,
   Though quite alive and quick,
Was indisposed. Another call
   Will make me deadly sick.

The Distich Writer

The distich writer seeks to please
  By being brief and quick.
But what's the use of brevity
  In a book three inches thick?

(VIII. 29)

To a Wooden Priapus

Mr. Priapus, scarecrow of
  No fructifying garden
Or vineyard, but of scanty woods
  The rude and homely warden—
The woods from which you came, from which
  Another can be born, too—
Keep hands of thieving knaves away
  From my poor trees, I warn you.
Protect them for my fireplace
  So I can warm my skin.
Remember, if my fire goes out,
  Then you, sir, will go in!

Fabulla

The only female friends she has
    Are old or ugly crows.
These she drags along with her
    To parties, visits, shows.

So it's no cause for wonder that
    Amidst such company
She's young, attractive, *beautiful*—
    Almost a joy to see!

(VIII. 79)

To Oppianus

Although you grab all invitations
    To dine out with friends,
You rant, you rail, you vilify,
    Disparage and condemn.

You'd better mend your manners and mend
    Your ways, however loath.
Be boorish or be gluttonous,
    But you cannot be both.

To an Old Friend

This friend whom your table procured for you
    And your banquets, so lavishly spread,
Do you really think that this new-found friend
    Is a friend when the truth is said?

It's the boar that you serve, and the mullet too,
    And the oysters he loves no end,
Not you; for if I were to dine as well
    He'd soon be my closest friend.

(IX. 14)

To the Emperor Domitian

I have (and may I have it long
    And long may you reign in Rome!)
A tiny country house nearby
    And a little city home.
And from the valley near my farm
    A curved pole and a pail
Supply my thirsty crops with drink,
    Though at no small travail.
My arid city house, however,
    Bemoans its lack of water
While the Aqua Marcia merrily feeds
    The fountains in this quarter.
The water which Your Majesty
    Will surely not withhold
From me will bring a Castalian Spring,
    Or another Shower of Gold.

To Sabellus

In countless poems you praise the charms
    Of Ponticus's pool—
Ponticus, the epicure.
    Unless I am a fool,
It's dinner, not a plunge, you crave,
    That's why you play it cool.

To Quintus on His Birthday

I wished to send you for your birthday
    A gift, a small thing really.
But you said, "No, I want no gift,"
    And meant it most sincerely.

Let both our wishes be esteemed.
    Why invite a rift
Between us? When *my* birthday comes,
    Please send *me* a gift.

(IX. 53)

To a Garland of Roses

Whether it was in Paestum or
The fields of Tivoli
That you were born, or Tusculum
Claims your nativity,
Or whether some country housewife culled you
In Praenestine fields,
Or whether you were among the splendors
Which Campania yields,
That to Sabinus you may seem
Fairer, a gift of more esteem,
Pretend, for it can do no harm,
You came from my Nomentum farm.

To Phoebus

The fact that only fairies ask you
    Home you can't conceal.
He who counts upon his "manhood"
    For his evening meal
Is himself no paragon
    Of manliness, I feel.

To Bluebeard Picentinus

Seven husbands in all she had.
   All died. I've some misgiving.
In marrying you, it must be true:
   Galla is tired of living!

To Aulus

The public likes my poems, though
A certain poet thinks them rough
Or never polished quite enough.

I could not care less! I prefer
The morsels served up in my books
To please my guests, not would-be cooks.

To Rufus

As long as you were hunting me,
   You sent me gifts as bait.
Once caught, I starved. You haven't sent
   A single thing of late.

To keep me caged, please keep on sending
   An appeasing gift,
Lest the boar grow ravenous
   And smash his cage and skip.

(IX. 88)

Coranus, Wine-Merchant

Not everywhere have heavy rains
   Harmed vintners or their vines.
Coranus filled a hundred jars—
   Of water for his wine!

On Paula

Paula wants to marry me,
   But I don't want to marry her.
She's too old for a boy like me.
   However, if this Paula were
Ninety-two or -three, let's say,
   I'd gladly marry her today!

(X. 8)

On Aper

It all was done, said he, in fun,
   While playing with his wealthy wife.
The arrow sped, and she was dead.
   Alas, the irony of life!
It all was done in a spirit of fun!
   A day's well ended that's well begun.

To Philaenis

Why do I walk with plastered chin
And white lead on my face,
You ask? I'll tell you, Phil, old pal,
To ward off your embrace.

On Marcus Antonius Primus
at Seventy-Five

With all the calm of saint and sage
He adds one more year to his age

And views the days and years long past
With soul serene, and unaghast

He sees approaching ever near
The waves of Lethe others fear.

No sad, unpleasant day can he
Recall, no day that should not be

With joy remembered, and with song.
A good man's life is doubly long,

For he lives twice who, day and night,
Can in his whole past take delight.

(X. 23)

To Sextilianus

The gift you used to send me once
    The middle of December
You've sent to a girl. The toga, too,
    You used to buy (remember?
Along about the first of March?)
    Has now become a gown
Leek-green and fancy for this girl
    To wear about the town.
These girls are yours for nothing now;
    Don't say I make no sense.
Look at it this way, please: these girls
    Are bought at my expense!

(X. 29)

To Phileros

Your seventh dowered wife has now
    Been buried in your field.
No farm in all this region has
    So lucrative a yield.

(X. 43)

On Happiness

These are the things, my handsome friend,
That make life happier to the end:

Wealth, not as an employee
Amassed, but as a legatee,

A farm responsive to my care,
A fire to warm my pensive chair,

Lawsuits never, rare the bane
Of dinner-suits, a mind that's sane,

A body sound, a shoulder free,
Not bowed by fear or slavery.

A disposition frank but kind,
Friends with me of an equal mind,

Friends who easily are led
To share my table plainly spread;

Wine at night the cares of day
To smile at and to chase away,

Fun and merriment in bed
But such as proper to those wed,

A sleep that makes the night on wings
Depart, and blessed daylight brings,

To be content with what we are,
And not to curse our natal star,

Never to fear the final day,
Never for death to hope and pray.

On Scorpus, the Charioteer

Scorpus am I, the favorite of the Circus,
  The rage and short-lived darling of all Rome.
Twenty-seven! The jealous Fates mistook
  My victories for my years, and called me home.

(X. 53)

To a Reader

If a poem of mine fills up a page,
   You pass it by. You'd rather read
The shorter, not the better ones.
   A feast to answer every need,

Rich and varied, and supplied
   With many viands widely drawn
From every shop, is offered you,
   And yet you glance at it with scorn,

The dainties only pleasing you.
   Fussy reader, away! Instead
Give me a guest who with his meal
   Must have some homely peasant bread.

(X. 59)

To the Schoolmaster

Master, spare your listless band!
  Do so, and may the best of joys
Befall you only in the land:
  Your class be largest, packed with boys

Who loudly chant their lucky lot
  And long their master's learning cry.
But summer's come, the days are hot,
  The grain, long ripened, tinder-dry.

So let the cat-o'-nine-tails rest
  That flogged old Marsyas cruelly
The day he rashly dared contest
  Apollo's long supremacy.

And let the threatening ferule rest—
  The master's scepter, sure to sober,
Sure to rouse up interest—
  Let it sleep until October.

It's not for long, my dear sir. Hell!
  Relax your standards! Summer's rough!
If in these dog days boys keep well,
  Kind sir, I'm sure they learn enough.

(X. 62)

To Theopompus

Who was so cruel, who forsook
His senses, making you a cook?
Who, heartless, could begrime a face
So fair as yours, who was so base
As to pollute and put to shame
Your locks with kitchen grease and flame?
Who but you is fit to dole
The wine from out the crystal bowl?
By whose hand mixed would Falernian wine
Smell sweeter and taste more divine?
If such sad fate as yours, in truth,
Awaits such beauteous, heavenly youth,
Then amorous Jupiter too will need
To make a cook of Ganymede.

To Caedicianus

Do you wonder why our friend
    Never goes to bed?
Well, look around! You see that hag?
    That's the one he wed.

To Polyclitus

Your glorious Juno, Polyclitus,
    Which Phidias might have envied you,
Would have conquered on Mount Ida
    Easily those other two,
Paris never hesitating
    Had she come into his view.
And surely had not Jupiter
    Known the Juno he adores,
He would certainly have fallen
    Quite in love with this of yours.

(X. 89)

To a Friend

No dragon, such as watched the Garden
　　Of the Hesperides,
Watches mine, the fruit whereof
　　Grows not with all the ease

With which it grew on the estate
　　Of that most favored king,
Alcinous of Phaeacia, one
　　Most blessed in everything!

Fearless of raids my little orchard
　　Puts forth hopeful leaves
But not much else. Its leaden fruit
　　Invites no hungry thieves.

These golden apples which I send you,
　　Juicy as they can be,
Are my own autumn's harvest of
　　The local grocery.

Numa

Just as the pyre was being laid
    With paper to get it started,
Just as his wife had bought the myrrh
    And home began to cart it,
Just when the grave was neatly dug
    For the bright urn newly fired,
Just as the bier was all prepared
    And the undertaker hired,
Just as Death above his head
    Appeared, and nearer hovered,
He named me heir. Then suddenly
    (Goddamn it!) he recovered!

(X. 97)

Epitaph on the Actor, Paris

Traveler on the Flaminian Way,
Do not hurry past, but stay.
Pause before this noble tomb
And read the sad, the dismal doom
That has befallen all the land:

The only man who could beguile
The world, the wit from Egypt's Nile,
The pride, the grief of Theater Rome,
The love of every hearth and home,
All grace and art personified
Were here interred when Paris died.

To Sabinus

Not every poem in this book
   Is to be read at night
When in your cups. You'll find some for
   The sober morning light.

(XI. 17)

On Aper

The house that Aper bought is such
    That even a hooting owl
Would scorn to haunt a place so old,
    So run-down, and so foul.

But wealthy Maro lives near by.
    The rest one can foretell:
Aper will dine superbly, though
    He will not lodge too well.

To Fabullus

You're much annoyed and wonder why
    I spurned your invitation.
It's caused you pain, and quite a bit
    Of needless irritation.

There were three hundred guests last night!
    And all of them unknown
To me. It's fun to dine with you,
    But not to dine alone!

(XI. 35)

To an Old Friend

You are rich and childless and very old.
　　Are your friends true friends? I'm sure
You have true friends, the ones you had
　　When you were young and poor.
The new-found friend's no true friend; why?
He longs for the day when you will die.

Lesbia

Lesbia swears she's never been had
    Gratis. That's true. You see:
When she is in one of her amorous moods,
    It's she who pays, not we.

Maro

You refuse to give me anything
  While you are still alive.
You tell me I'll be taken care of
  After you have died.
If that's the way things are, my friend,
I hope you come to a speedy end.

To Parthenopaeus

To soothe your throat so long inflamed
   By a cough that does not end,
Honey, nuts, and little cakes
   Your doctor recommends,

As if to soothe a crying child.
   Still you cough constantly;
Your cough is not a cough at all,
   But simple gluttony.

To Charidemus

When you were rich, your only care
    Was the pursuit of men,
The young, the handsome ones. You took
    No note of women then.

Old women now are your concern.
    The wonders hardship can
Perform! You once were quite a queer.
    Today you're quite a man!

(XI. 87)

To Zoïlus

He who called you vicious
Was stupid, or he lied.
You're not vicious, Zoïlus.
You're vice personified.

On the Poet Theodorus

Not a single trace remains
  Of poet Theodorus' home.
Everything completely burned,
  Every last poetic tome!

You Muses and Apollo too,
  Now are you fully satisfied?
O monstrous shame that when it burned
  The poet was not trapped inside!

(XI. 93)

To Safronius

You are so pure in mind and heart,
   In aspect, too, so mild,
I wonder that you ever could
   Implant your wife with child.

Africanus

Here's a man who's wangled millions;
    Yet the parasite's not done.
Fortune gives too much to many,
    Yet, strange to say, enough to none.

Themison

Do you ask, dear reader, why Themison
  Has no wife? Why, hell!
The reason's rather obvious:
  His sister does as well!

To Aper

You're always sober, never drunk.
   Such temperance is fine
In servants and domestics, but
   Not in a friend of mine.

On His Home in Spain

This grove, this spring, this cooling shade
Of woven vines and branches made,
This stream that irrigates my fields,
This meadow, this little bed that yields,
Like Paestum, roses twice a year,
These vegetables that never fear
The winter's frost but ever grow
In neat green order, row on row,
These friendly eels that swim and swerve
Within their own fresh-water preserve,
This snow-white dovecote where alight
The birds that grace it, equally white,
All these come from my patroness.
To me returned from all the press
And stress of life in busy Rome
Marcella gave me for my own
This house as well as this domain
In Bilbilis in sunny Spain.
Even if Nausicaä named
Me owner of her father's famed
Rich fields and kingdom widely known,
I'd tell him I prefer my own.

To Julius Martialis

If rightly I remember,
   If rightly I recall,
The count is four and thirty years
   Of friendship—summers all!

Though joys were mixed with sorrows
   That tried our friendship sore,
Yet weighed against each other, sure
   The joys were rather more.

Let him who would escape them,
   The pain, the bitterness,
Be no man's friend. He'll know less grief
   And far less happiness.

(XII. 34)

To Callistratus

You tell me, buddy, you've been used
    Quite often like a whore.
Whoever dares reveal such things
    Conceals, I'm sure, much more.

To Pontilianus

You lie, and I believe you.
  I praise your wretched verse.
You sing, I sing. You drink, I drink.
  You break wind, I converse

Right on, revealing nothing
  Of what I'm quite aware
You've done. We play, I always lose.
  There's only one affair

At which I'm never present,
  Of which I never say
A word. And still I've not received
  A thing up till this day.

"I'll give you something special,
  My friend," you say, "when I
Am gone." I don't want anything
  But this: I wish you'd die!

To a Friend

There's something easy, difficult,
Hard and soft about you
All the time. I cannot live
With you or without you.

To Aulus

Do you wonder why some sharper always
    Manages to outwit
Fabullinus? Honest men
    Are bait for hypocrites.

To Polycharmus

You take to your bed, sir, apparently sick,
   Ten times a year, even more,
And you're never the slightest bit worse for it all.
   Your friends are the sufferers, for
As often as you get up out of your bed
   Recovered, you've always the gall
To ask for a glad-you-are-well-again gift.
   Get good and sick once and for all!

To Cinna

A handsome boy, who far outshines
   In face and curls his other slaves,
Fair though they are, our Cinna's made
   His cook. O Cinna, you hungry knave!

(XII. 64)

Warning

When the heavy Spartan discus hurtles,
   Gleaming, whirling through the air,
Boys, move away! Let it kill but once:
   When it killed Hyacinthus, the young, the fair.

To Zeus

I wonder why, Olympian Zeus,
    Danaë obtained her price,
While Leda, who was just as good,
    Was good for nothing and as nice.

On Propertius' Monobiblos

Cynthia, the lyric theme
   Of young Propertius' eloquence,
Gained immortality from him,
   And gave him a name no less immense.

On the Dedication of the Colosseum in Rome

Barbaric Egypt, boast no more
   The wonders of your pyramids!
Babylon, vaunt no longer now
   The gardens of Semiramis!
Let not the soft Ionians swell
   With pride for their great Artemis
Whose temple splendor long has been
   The claim and fame of Ephesus.
Let Delos hide its head in shame
   And say no more Apollo
Himself did rear the altar there
   (A claim both weak and hollow).
Let not the Carians wildly praise
   The wondrous, sculptured tomb
The Queen at Halicarnassus raised
   When Mausolus met his doom.
Let every wonder of the past
   Yield now to this great wonder.
Fame shall cling to this at last,
   Her applause as loud as thunder.

To His Book

Whoa, there! Whoa, there! That's enough!
　　We've come now to the end,
And still you itch to gallop on
　　(Though I wish to descend),
As if your race were not yet run
　　Which was quite done indeed
The day you started. Even now
　　The reader moans, the speed
Is too exhausting. The printer, too,
　　Complains the ride's been rough
And cries, "Slow down, slow down there, now!
　　Whoa, there! That's enough!"

Notes

I. 2   *Minerva's Forum.* Actually, the Forum Nervae, which contained a temple of Pallas Athena (Minerva); hence Martial calls it the Forum Palladium.

that of Peace. The Forum Pacis, also known as the Forum Vespasiani.

I. 107   *Virgil.* Publius Virgilius Maro (70–19 B.C.), the greatest of the Roman poets, author of the *Aeneid.*

Maecenas. Wealthy literary patron during the reign of Augustus. Both Virgil and Horace were members of his literary circle and were indebted to him for patronage.

Horace. Quintus Horatius Flaccus (65–8 B.C.), famous lyric poet, author of the *Odes* and *Epodes*, friend of Virgil.

II. 21   *practices.* Probably a reference to that of *fellatio.*

II. 22   *sisters nine.* The nine Muses, goddesses of the arts and of literature.

Apollo. In Greek mythology, the god of music, archery, and prophecy. He is frequently represented in art as playing the lyre in the company of the nine Muses.

II. 42   See note on II. 21.

II. 90   *Quintilian.* Marcus Fabius Quintilianus (*ca.* A.D. 35–*ca.* 95), celebrated teacher, author of the *Institutio Oratoria.*

Scopas. Eminent Greek sculptor of the fourth century B.C.

III. 35   *Phidias.* Famous Athenian architect and sculptor (*fl.* fifth century B.C.), who, among other things, supervised the building and the sculptures of the Parthenon.

III. 39   *Ganymede.* In Greek mythology, a handsome Trojan youth who was carried off by Zeus's eagle and taken to Olympus, where he was made Zeus's cupbearer.

III. 41   *Mentor.* Among the ancients, the most famous artist in embossing silver. Martial often refers to him.

III. 45 *Thyestes' banquet table*. In Greek mythology, Atreus, father of Agamemnon and Menelaus, invited his brother Thyestes to a banquet at which he served Thyestes the flesh of his own children. For the full story, see Lempriere's *Classical Dictionary* (London: Routledge and Kegan Paul, 1948).

III. 56 *a well*. Both the Greeks and the Romans usually drank their wine mixed with water.

III. 64 *the Sirens*. In Greek mythology, birds with heads of women, whose alluring songs drew passing sailors to approach their island, where they were destroyed. Ulysses, to escape this destruction, put wax in his sailors' ears and had himself tied to the mast. For the full story, see Homer's *Odyssey*, Book XII.

Canius. Canius Rufus, poet, orator, and humorist, friend of Martial.

IV. 44 *Vesuvius*. The volcano that erupted on August 24, A.D. 79, destroying Pompeii, Herculaneum, and Stabiae. The account of this eruption by Pliny the Younger (Ep. 6, 16, and 20) is famous.

Bacchus (also known as Dionysus). In Greek mythology, the god of wine and fertility.

satyrs. Followers of Bacchus. They are generally depicted as humans with the tail of a horse.

Aphrodite. In Greek mythology, the goddess of love and beauty, identified by the Romans with Venus.

Laecedaemonian island. According to Hesiod, Aphrodite ("foam-born") rose from the sea and landed first at Cythera, an island near the Laecedaemonian coast.

Geryones. Also, in the singular, Geryon. In Greek mythology, a monster who lived in the far west. He was slain by Hercules, who drove his oxen back all the way to Greece.

IV. 49 *Tereus*. In Greek mythology, husband of Procne, who, in revenge for his having violated her sister Philomela and cut out her tongue, served him for supper the flesh of their son Itys. For a full account of this famous story, see Lempriere.

Thyestes. See note on III. 45 above.

Daedalus. To escape from the island of Crete, Daedalus fashioned for himself and for his son Icarus wings made of feathers and wax.

Polyphemus. The one-eyed Cyclops blinded by Ulysses. For the full story see Homer's *Odyssey*, Book XIX.

IV. 54   *crown of gold.* Bestowed upon Collinus in A.D. 86 for having won first prize in a poetry contest, the *agon Capitolinus.*

the Sisters. The three Fates (Clotho, Lachesis, and Atropos), usually represented as spinning, measuring, and cutting the thread of life.

V. 10   *that temple.* The temple of Jupiter on the Capitol, restored in 62 B.C. by Quintus Lutatius Catulus.

Ennius. Quintus Ennius (239–169 B.C.), one of the greatest of the early Roman poets. He wrote tragedies and an epic called the *Annales.* Only fragments of these and other works survive.

Virgil. See note on I. 107 above.

Menander's plays. Menander (*ca.* 342–292 B.C.), the most famous of the New Comedy writers. He had a tremendous influence on Plautus and Terence, who, in turn, had a deep influence on European comedy.

Corinna. A woman who figures prominently in Ovid's love poems, the *Amores.*

Ovid's works. In addition to the *Amores* Ovid (Publius Ovidius Naso, 43 B.C.–A.D. 18) wrote the *Ars Amatoria*, the *Heroides*, the *Fasti*, the *Tristia*, and the famous *Metamorphoses.*

V. 34   *hound of Hades.* Cerberus, the three-headed dog that guarded the entrance to the lower world.

V. 39   *Croesus.* The last King of Lydia (560–546 B.C.), whose wealth has become proverbial. The very exciting story of Croesus is told in Herodotus' *The Persian Wars*, I, 26–33.

the beggar Irus. A character who appears in Homer's *Odyssey*, Book XVIII.

V. 41   *Attis.* A Phrygian shepherd who, driven mad by Cybele, the mother of the gods, castrated himself and died. From that time on the priests of Cybele castrated themselves to maintain their vows of chastity. For a more detailed account, see Lempriere.

V. 64   *summer's snow.* The Romans, during the summer, cooled their wine by draining it through snow which they brought from the mountains.

Mausoleum. Erected by Augustus for his own use and that of his family. Significant remains of it survive in Rome.

V. 67   *Procne.* See note on IV. 49 above.

V. 76   *a famous King.* Mithridates, King of Pontus. See A. E. Housman's famous reference to him in *A Shropshire Lad*, lxii.

VII. 15   *Hylas.* In Greek mythology, a handsome boy who accompanied Hercules on the quest for the Golden Fleece. When the Argonauts stopped at Cios, Hylas was sent ashore for water. He never returned. The water-nymphs of the island, in love with his beauty, pulled him down into the spring. Hercules went ashore to look for him, delaying so long that the Argonauts sailed without him.
Naiads. Female personifications of streams, lakes, and rivers.

VII. 21   *Lucan.* Roman poet (A.D. 39–65), author of the *Pharsalia*, an unfinished epic. Suspected of having taken part in Piso's conspiracy against Nero, he was ordered to commit suicide.

VII. 73   *Esquiline, Aventine.* Two of the seven hills of Rome.
widowed Cybele. Because her beloved Attis is dead. See note on V. 41.

VIII. 40   *Priapus.* In Greek mythology, son of Dionysus and Aphrodite, god of the fruitfulness of the field. His statues, rude *hermae* made of wood, were placed in gardens.

IX. 18   *Aqua Marcia.* One of the aqueducts in Rome.
Castalian Spring. A spring on Mt. Parnassus, sacred to Apollo and the Muses. Poets believed its waters gave poetic inspiration.

X. 23   *Lethe.* The river of forgetfulness, in Hades.

X. 62   *Marsyas.* In Greek mythology, the satyr who became so proficient at playing the flute that he dared to challenge Apollo to a musical contest. Marsyas lost, and Apollo punished him by tying him to a tree and flaying him alive.

X. 66   *Ganymede.* See note on III. 39.

X. 89   *Polyclitus.* Fifth-century Greek sculptor, one of the most celebrated of antiquity. Two of his famous statues (the Doryphoros and the Diadumenos) exist in replicas. As a sculptor. Polyclitus is considered second only to Phidias.

Mount Ida. Located near Troy, the site of the famous beauty contest (the Judgment of Paris). The contestants were Juno, Minerva, and Venus. Venus was awarded the prize, the golden apple.

X. 94 *Garden of the Hesperides.* In Greek mythology, a celebrated garden in which grew the golden apples given to Juno by Jupiter on her wedding day. These apples were guarded by the Hesperides (three maidens, daughters of Hesperus) and by a dragon. One of the twelve labors of Hercules was to bring back some of these golden apples.

Alcinous. King of Phaeacia. His famous orchard was a place where the "fruit never fails nor runs short, winter and summer alike. It comes at all seasons of the year, and there is never a time when the West Wind's breath is not assisting, here the bud, and here the ripening fruit; so that pear after pear, apple after apple, cluster on cluster of grapes, and fig upon fig are always coming to perfection" (Homer's *Odyssey*, Book VII, E. V. Rieu's translation).

XI. 13 *Flaminian Way.* The famous northern road that led from Rome to Ariminium (modern Rimini). Wealthy Romans built magnificent mausolea along this and other roads leading out of Rome.

XII. 31 *Marcella.* Martial's friend who, when he returned to his birthplace Bilbilis, gave him an estate to live on.

XIV. 164 *Hyacinthus.* In Greek mythology, a handsome youngster who lived near Sparta. He was accidentally killed while he and Apollo were hurling the discus.

XIV. 175 *Zeus.* In Greek mythology, the supreme ruler of the gods. The major gods were said to have lived on Mt. Olympus.
Danaë. In Greek mythology, daughter of Acrisius. Zeus fell in love with her and visited her in a shower of gold, sometimes depicted by writers and painters as a shower of gold coins.
Leda. In Greek mythology, wife of Tyndareus. Zeus fell in love with her, as well, and approached her in the shape of a swan.

XIV. 189 *Propertius.* Famous Roman love poet (*ca.* 50–*ca.* 16 B.C.). He wrote four books of elegies, the first called *Monobiblos*, a collection of poems, many of which were addressed to Cynthia, the beautiful woman he was in love with for a time. The publication of this first book of elegies brought Propertius immediate fame.

L.S. 1 *Artemis*. In Greek mythology, daughter of Zeus and Leto, and sister of Apollo. Identified by the Romans with Diana, goddess of the chase and wild life. One of her most famous temples was erected in Ephesus.

Delos. In Greek mythology, the island on which Apollo and his sister Artemis were born. The altar of Apollo there was made of horns of animals which Artemis had slain. This altar was considered one of the seven wonders of the world.

the wondrous sculptured tomb. The amazingly beautiful tomb (Mausoleum) which Artemisia, Queen of Halicarnassus, built for her husband Mausolus. The statue of Mausolus and some of the sculpture for this tomb are in the British Museum.